SUCCEED IN LOTTO

EVEN IF YOU DON'T KNOW WHERE TO START!

Rational investors get the best edge and
odds in a lotto or lottery system.
Run a syndicate (pool) and deal with taxes.

DR. SCOTT BROWN

WORRY FREE WEALTH

How to Succeed at Lotto Even if you Don't Know Where to Start.

Kindle & Interior design and preparation by Soumi Goswami.

Contact Soumi directly at soumi.goswami.pub@gmail.com

Table of Contents

Goals:

At the end of this course, students will be able to…

1. Understand and employ the most powerful scientifically proven lottery wheeling systems on the planet.
2. Intelligently establish a single family or multi-family system for lifelong lottery play fun and guaranteed prizes.
3. Intelligently establish a lottery syndicate (pool).
4. Set forth and follow a pre-planned process should you win millions.

Who should (or should not) take this course?

If you are considering or are already playing the lottery you should take this course.

What will students need to know or do before starting this course?

A basic understanding of simple arithmetic is useful but not necessary.

Section 1 • Doc Brown Welcomes You!

Welcome to Lottery Systems!

Discover how to **get the most** out of this course. For special offers go to http://worryfreewealth.com/offers/

Introduction: How Bad Do You Want to Win?

I am **Dr. Scott Brown**. I hold a Ph.D. in finance from the University of South Carolina. I am a professor of finance of the AACSB accredited **Graduate School of Business** of the **University of Puerto Rico**.

Just 5% of all business schools in the world enjoy **AACSB accreditation**.

MBA degrees from these schools are **highly prized**.

Why Did I Create This Course? What is it All About? Why is it Important?

My brother owns a gas station and sells tickets in California for the state and Mega Millions lotto. A friend of ours from high school won a million in the California Lotto.

A lightning strike that close to home got my attention.

I discovered that people were teaming up to play more numbers, and thus more tickets. I wondered if there was anything to the wheeling systems out there.

Marisol and I picked up Gail Howard's book on Amazon. Then we paid a few hundred dollars for her wheeling software.

I discovered that it is a lot of work to fill out lottery tickets. And it is a hassle to buy and redeem a lot of lottery tickets.

But if you work at it you will find ways like we did to stay in the game.

Today we follow a simple system that costs us $10 per week to make sure that we have a single random ticket working in our local Puerto Rico Loto Plus and Powerball draws twice a week.

Puerto Rico Loto Plus costs us $2 total. That's $1 for the main draw and two 50¢ entries into a reserve pool and multiplier. Powerball costs us $2 for the main draw and $1 for a Power play multiplier for a total of $3 per ticket.

There are 52.1429 weeks in a year. That means that we play a total of $521.43 annually.

We will invest $20,857.16 over a 40-year time span. Our system will be ahead if we hit a smaller prize or sequence of prizes in the Power Ball or Puerto Rico Loto Plus to net more than $20,857.16 after tax.

That would put us on the house's money so to speak.

We can invest in lotto because we max out our retirement plans each year with savings. We play fully loaded tickets. But we could just play the main draws for $6 a week.

That would reduce our cost to $312.86; a savings of $156.43 a year.

This would amount to $12,514.40 over 40 years and a savings of $6,257.04.

Who is This Course For?

Our retirement plans offer no investment that could make us hundreds of millions overnight. Only a large lottery can.

Our lottery tickets are equivalent to extremely deep out of the money calls with extraordinary payoff possibilities. But again, such calls do not exist in equities.

Marisol and I cannot ever hope to turn a $2.00 investment in stock options, futures, futures options, forex, or forex options to land us a $1,586.4 billion-dollar record prize in Powerball that just three people won in California, Florida and Tennessee.

And for that reason, we view a lottery ticket as an investment.

But only because we max out our retirement savings. If you are not at least maxing out your Roth IRA and piling in up to the matching on your employer sponsored 401(k) just read and listen.

Do not start buying lottery tickets until you are managing your retirement plans properly and contributing maximally.

Ditto for forming a lottery syndicate. Do not invest in or form a lottery syndicate until you are maxing out your retirement plans.

This course is for you if you are a healthy retirement saver who is looking for alternative possibilities of enhancing your family wealth.

In This Training, You Will Learn. . .

Section 2: The Surprising History of Lotto and Lottery. I was amazed to discover as I researched this course that the Catholic church financed some of the great tourist attractions today with lotteries in the dark ages.

Section 3: What Academics Know About Lottery and Lotto. You'll discover bizarre factoids such as the numbers Joe the Plumber hates to play. Play these and you reduce your risk of sharing the jackpot.

Section 4: A Guide to Avoiding Scams and Delusions. Avoid pseudo experts and cons alike trying to grab your money you could otherwise use to play lotto.

Section 5: The Best Lottery System in the World. Discover how to put the hard science of Bluskov wheeling systems to work for your family or lottery syndicate today.

Section 6: Death and Taxes. If you should win a major jackpot these guidelines will keep you out of trouble.

What's in This for You? Is This Right for You? Answer These 6 Vital Questions!

Do you want to…

1. Decrease your probability of sharing a prize or jackpot?
2. Play more numbers than five plus a bonus?
3. Increase the number of smaller prizes?
4. Tap into small prize guarantees?
5. Explore the possibility of forming a lottery syndicate?
6. Double check to make sure that you are playing lottery correctly?

At the end of this course you will be the most knowledgeable in your circle on lottery guaranteed. But first go to this important page now to enroll in a special offer of 50% off ($20 normally, get for -> $10) on the Udemy course corresponding to this book that gives you videos and exams as well as direct access to me::

https://www.udemy.com/succeed-in-lotto-even-if-you-dont-know-where-to-start/?couponCode=KINDLE-LOTTO

Section 2 • The History of Lottery

Amazing facts regarding the birth of lotto and lottery!

A Brief History of Lotto and Lottery

Economics professor Gerald Willmann of Stanford University explains that Moses was the first known to use a lottery to distribute land as lots. Read his article *"The History of Lotteries"* from 1999 for more. The term is still used in real estate to designate a parcel of land.

Lotteries are odd social activities. People should not be willing to place money into an uncertain bet when the mathematical expected outcome of the lottery ticket is nearly a sure loss.

A large body of literature started by Friedman and Savage in 1948 has offered a reasonable explanation of why people willingly seek negative expected utility. We will explore this academic puzzle later in this course.

The word lot comes from German *"hleut."* English is heavily derived from German.

The Germanic tribes had a great deal of influence on the English language to do trade, migration and warfare with the British Isles. The English evolution of the German word is lot.

French is also influenced by German. Lot is also used in French for *"hleut."*

In Spanish, the word is *"lote."* The word was transformed into lottery by either the Italians or the Dutch.

Lottery is defined as *"a procedure for distributing something among a group of people by lot or chance."* It is further described as *"a form of gambling in which a usually large number of people purchase chances, called lottery tickets."* Professor Willmann explains that lotteries have been used to allocate "anything from property rights to punishments by chance."

Lotteries have been used throughout history to allocate, assign, or settle:

- Property rights.
- Unpopular (bad) jobs.
- Legal disputes.

Moses distributed property rights, and Jonah was sacrificed to the sea by lottery in the old testament. The Koran (Quran) forbids any form of gambling. If you ever work in Saudi Arabia as Tom Hanks does in the movie Hologram for a King don't look for a national lottery.

There is none.

The philosopher Cicero criticized Roman oracle lotteries as corrupt. Tiles were selected from a pool and the inscriptions were interpreted after a question was posed to the Sibylline Oracles.

Augustus used lotteries for pleasure to distribute gifts to guests. Nero threw thousands of lottery tickets to the public. Prizes could be real estate, ships, or slaves.

Hedonistic Roman emperor Heliogabalus allowed lotteries their heyday in the third century. By this time most of the lottery prizes were worthless.

Lotteries fell to the wayside from this point in the history of the Roman empire.

The Lottery reappears in the 13th century in Brussels to allocate market space. It is used as the Gottesurteil in Germany as a mechanism for dispensing justice in the 16th century. This was such a bizarre and unreasoning form of justice that the church outlawed it in the 12th century.

Belgium and the Netherlands used lotteries to finance fortifications, churches, or to increase the town treasury.

The Dutch in the low country created the class lottery in the 15th century. The number and nature of prizes and ticket prices and quantities were set in advance analogous to scratcher tickets today. Numbers (Pick 2, Pick 3, Pick 4) share aspects of both lotto and class lotteries. Prizes were raffled off in a series of drawings from least to highest prize value.

This insured that the lottery organizer faced no risk.

Jumping late into the lottery required paying for prior draws. Sometimes only one drawing was held but all other features of a class lottery were present.

While the Dutch developed their class system the Italians developed a lottery called the "Bianca carta."

Heavily promoted drawings for prizes were entered by paying for a card. The few winning cards were far outnumbered by white blanks.

Five Genua key positions were drawn by lottery from 90 senators. Lotto formed as the public began betting on the outcome.

Caterina de Medici brought the game of Bianca carta from Italy when she married King Henry II of France. The name morphed into Blanque, replacing the Italian word for white with that of the French.

This was not new to the French.

King Francis I extended the lottery to France before Caterina. His friend Jean Laurent operated the first lottery in France in 1539 paying the king 2,000 francs a year. This was the first form of legalized gambling in France.

Some form of French government lottery has operated for 471 years since. Today the Lotto and Euro Millions runs under the Francaise des Jeux (FCAU) government authority.

The lottery helped restore the French budget and clawed capital back from foreign lotteries. French citizens were routinely participating in Italian lotteries because France had none before Laurent.

Lotteries are infrequently used to finance a bridge (unsuccessfully) in Italy and a hospital in France during the 1600s. King Louis the Fourteenth gave out three thousand lottery tickets to the ladies of the court. He himself won valuable prizes he gave back after outcry.

The city of Lyon helped the poor with a lottery in 1699 as popularity of the game returned. The Municipality of Paris established a lottery by royal decree in 1700.

Churches picked up on the financing trend. Most renovations from 1714 to 1729 were paid for by lottery proceeds.

The birth of the regular lottery came forth from pity on the poor. The lottery of the Hôpital de la Pitié was the first in 1754. The far larger Ecole Militaire regular lottery came in 1757.

Drawings were held monthly based on the Italian Lotto design.

The French lottery was monopolized by King Louis in the 16th century to cover a 37 million livres government spending deficit. All other lotteries were absorbed.

This produced around 10 million livres per year.

A Brief History of Lotto and Lottery

The lottery fell out of favor and was abolished by November of 1793 in the aftermath of the French revolution. But the demand to play did not fall and players bought tickets in foreign lotteries such as that of nearby Cologne in Germany.

In 1798 the Loterie Nationale was reestablished by the revolutionary government. It languished from competition until 1804 when Napoléon made one of his generals a director. State profits soared from 15 to 24 million.

The French Emperor forced the establishment of a Loterie Nationale in each country he conquered. This spurred the growth of profits. Pontifical lotteries were replaced by the Loterie Nationale in key cities.

- Brussels
- Turin
- Genua
- Florence

- Hamburg
- Rome

Napoléon was a surprisingly efficient governor. The Loterie Nationale was very well organized.

This shows in the financials. A full 20% went to the state and 70% in prizes. Just 10% of the take was used for administration.

The beginning of the end of the French National Lottery came in 1814 when territorial losses for the French generated the first loss. The July monarchy shut down the lottery in 1836 when the state budget stabilized.

This is an example of a historic pattern throughout history.

Lotteries come into political favor when the state faces budgetary crisis. The game loses its appeal when governments are flush with cash.

France would not have a lottery until almost a full century later in 1933.

The New York Lottery

Latin America had a lottery in the pioneer days. English colonial lottery tickets were sold in North America while the Spanish colonial lottery ran to the south.

New York created its first public lottery in 1746. This financed city fortifications. This first was unsuccessful. A second raised money for Columbia University which was first named Kings College in honor of Cambridge across the pond in England.

A lottery raised money for firearms for the poor during the French and Indian war. Then another built the jail for prisoners of the same war.

Yet another lottery in Albany covered wartime debts in 1758.

A 1751 lottery built the Sandy Hook lighthouse, the oldest in the United States. The burden of war made taxes out of the question.

Another in the same year repaired the New York City Hall.

Two years later a lottery subsidized the farming of hemp — a non-psychoactive form of Cannabis used for rope and textiles. This was intended to reduce the trade deficit with England.

Lotteries were formed by legislation and were advertised daily in local newspapers.

The success of public lotteries spurred the formation of private games. These competed with public lotteries aimed at improving a social asset.

Laws become more restrictive for privateering in lottery as the government clamped down.

England banned public lotteries in 1721 and New York followed with similar legislation in the same year. This did not deter lottery privateers. In 1747 a fine was levied on private lotteries of twice the handle.

Half of the fine went to the litigant and half to the state.

The sale of tickets of other colonies in New York was banned in 1759.

Liquidation of property through private lotteries became illegal in 1772. Penalties for running a private lottery were increased in 1774.

A lottery to finance fire buckets in 1780 and another to fund the needs of refugees was held in 1781 during the American revolution.

The first lottery after the revolution repaired the city hall of New York to prepare it to become the seat of Congress. Then in 1795 a lottery helped the poor. A 1797 lottery improved the roads.

The start of the 19th century sparked the lotteries for these public works:

- Improved Hudson River Navigation.
- Encouragement of Literature.
- Road Along Black River.

- Endowment of Union College (Founded in 1795, this was the first college chartered by the Board of Regents of the State of New York).
- Construction of the New York State Capital.

By this time the organization of lotteries became big business. Lottery managers had to be bonded but made fat commissions of 10 to 15%. They made more money selling tickets to lottery offices in bulk.

These offices made a fat margin. Lotteries ran for days and offices rented out tickets for specific days. This was cheaper than buying a ticket that spanned all days of the drawing.

Then the office also sold insurance on tickets to recoup blanks (losers). Public lottery insurance was made illegal in 1807 and in 1809 began to apply to private lotteries.

The first lottery manager failed in 1807 incurring a loss of more than $40,000 as New York covered prizes with state taxes.

Nonetheless new lotteries appeared such as that which funded the creation of a botanic garden for medical science. This became the Elgin Botanic Gardens. Public opposition to gambling generated stronger laws prohibiting private lotteries and lottery insurance in 1813.

Some lotteries persisted such as various for Union College. Allegations of fraud by lottery office proprietor Charles Baldwin led to the conviction of the manager of the Medical Science lottery sparking 1819 legislations stipulating internal regulations and standards imposed on lottery managers.

The New York state constitution was passed in 1820 with stipulations that the legislature should not have the authority to authorize lotteries.

Nonetheless state legislatures authorized two more lotteries in 1820 for the city of Albany and in 1823 for a fever hospital in New York. In 1822 an act was passed entitled *"An act to limit the continuance of lotteries."*

This transferred the risk of prior legislated lotteries that were still running. The literature lotteries were assigned to agents Yates and M'Intyre who had to accept the risks of running the lottery as a business.

The last lottery act was passed in 1826 to increase penalties for forging and unauthorized ticket sales.

Allegations that Yates and M'Intyre sold more tickets than authorized led to a settlement with the New York state legislature in 1933.

This was the tipping point. All lotteries ceased by the end of that year.

Lotteries in The Old German States

The first German lottery was held in 1470 in Augsberg. Then came one in Strasburg (1473), Erfurt (1477), Gemünden in 1480, and various in Nürmberg in 1487. Frankfurt on Main held a lottery in 1506 and another in Osnabrück in 1521.

The Hamburg lottery operated for money in 1610 as the beginning of a series of well-run class lotteries. The Hamburg Senate referenced the success of the Dutch lotteries. Friedrichstadt was the next (clearly Dutch) derived auction. The town itself looks more Dutch than German.

Berlin adopted a class lottery in 1703.

Prussia expanded this into a national lottery in 1763. Friedrich the Great illegalized out-of-state and private lotteries to enhance revenue.

Munich followed in 1783 as class lotteries sprung up throughout Germany in more than twenty cities. The first Lotto magazine was established in Hamburg.

Lotto fell out of favor as Hamburg closed the game in 1785, By 1861 Lotto was no longer running in Germany. Lotto was much more controversial than a class lottery.

All were closed by 1861.

German unification a decade later in 1871 allowed the Prussian government to set up bi-lateral laws that segmented state governments.

Regional class lotteries could only sell to their local market but the National lottery could sell anywhere in Germany.

The words lotto and lottery are used interchangeably but the difference between lotto and class lottery is important.

A class lottery is a process for distributing prizes by lot with one or more pre-printed tickets bearing numbers drawing preassigned prizes. Players do not select numbers when playing a class lottery.

All other tickets are blanks. Americans often call this a raffle.

Scratchers are another modern example.

Lotto is a game of chance like bingo where numbers are randomly selected from a rotating spherical cage with numbered ping-pong balls. In this case the players select their own numbers.

This course focuses on strategies to optimize lotto play.

Saxony, Hamburg, and Brunswick resisted Prussian authority until the Nazis merged them in 1938 with the Gleischschaltung that synchronized all of Germany's economic and social function under totalitarian control. The end of the war in 1945 halted all lotteries in Gemany.

Four class lotteries were established in post-war Germany in 1947 and 1948.

- The Munich Süddeutsch Klassenlotterie.
- The Hamburg Norddeutsche Klassenlotterie.
- The Koblenz Klassenlotterie des Landes Rheinland-Pfalz
- The Berlin Deustsche Klassenlotterie

The Berlin class lottery was merged with that of Hamburg when the wall went up between east and west.

Western Germany introduced the Zahlenlotto developed a year before in Berlin. This offered up different probabilities based on picking 6 from 49 rather than 5 from 90 numbers on Saturdays.

Lotto took over the market as class lotteries stagnated. A third game offered 7 from 38 numbers in 1982.

The Modern History of Lotteries

In 1933 France reestablished the national lottery. In 1956 the Association Intenatinoale de Loteries d'Etats was created and meets biennially to create an international lottery.

The funds would be ear tagged to develop underdeveloped countries through education. Competition from foreign lotteries has impeded this path.

This was not supported by the major markets in the U.S. and the U.K. where lotteries were banned at the time. The initiative collapsed.

The U.S. created lotteries in the 1980s. Most other countries in the world have lotteries.

More than three hundred lotteries have emerged since the fall of the Soviet Union. Most are run by the Russian mafia.

Despite this Russia ran a fascinating lottery where the winner got a stay on the space station.

History shows that people have mixed reactions to lotteries. Nobody forces anybody to play.

When the state is fat with cash lotteries tend to be judged as bad. When private interests make gobs of money the state steps in to monopolize and politicians promote the game as good.

The states of the union in America rapidly shifted to support of the lottery when strapped for cash. In this sense the state vigorish costs gamblers 50% of the price of a ticket.

The vigorish is the percent of the handle the state keeps.

The poor spend a larger percentage of income on gambling and play more numbers as well as scratcher class lottery tickets. Thus, state lottery earnings are a regressive tax on the poor.

Contrary to the belief of some, the lottery is centuries old and has been a fixture of life for many millennia.

Section 3 • Academics Who Know More than a 5th Grader!

What some of the greatest economic minds have to say about lottery.

Pari-mutuel Betting Markets: Racetracks and Lotteries

Finance Professor Richard Thaler of the University of Chicago and Bill Ziemba of the University of British Columbia published a useful article that helps explain why people play lottery — a game that returns 50 cents on the dollar at best. They discuss the strategy of playing "against the crowd" in lotto.

Playing this strategy increases the expected value of a bet over a strategy of choosing numbers at random. Here is how it works.

The choice to play a game you expect to lose over and over throughout your life is an irrational choice within the framework of standard economics.

Researchers point out that betting markets are ideal for studying rational financial behavior and market efficiency. This is because each bet has a final termination date — unlike a share of stock.

The quick-repeat feedback of wagering markets is highly conducive to learning.

Both racetrack betting and lotto-type lottery games are pari-mutuel betting markets. The history of lottery games per this study includes Christ's robe which was given to a lottery winner so that it would not have to be cut.

Lotteries paid for the construction of the Sistine Chapel and its paintings.

The Italian lottery has been running since 1530. Lottery is played in over 100 countries today. Harvard, Princeton, and Yale were partially funded by lotteries.

The debts of Thomas Jefferson were fulfilled by lottery.

Corruption led to the collapse of lottery in America and Canada. It was restarted in 1964 in New Hampshire and in 1967 in Montreal. Sales and popularity of lotto games have exploded despite an expected return (payout rate) of between 40 and 60 cents on the dollar.

This is a poor investment for a rational investor. Hence the popularity of lotto is puzzling.

Nonetheless, researchers ask the question, *"is it possible to obtain positive expected value bets in lotto games?"*

The article explains that not all numbers in a lottery form panel are equally popular with the public. Professor Chernoff of M.I.T. was the first to exploit non-random public betting patterns in 1980.

His report is *"An Analysis of the Massachusetts Numbers Game."*

Chernoff discovered that people don't like numbers ending with 0 or 9 and the number 8 to a lesser degree. This suggested that there could exist combinations with positive expected values.

However, Chernoff's students lost attempting to play good numbers.

They were unlucky in that unpopular numbers came up less frequently than forecasted. And they had insufficient bankroll to continue over the long haul — a problem known as "gambler's ruin."

The base of the lotto system in the United States is 6/49. The probability of winning is one in 13,983,816.

Considering that the game plays twice a week you have just 104 opportunities per year.

Dividing the probability by opportunities to play per year reveals that it would take 134,360 years to fully expect to win.

Therefore, rational economics fails to explain why people gamble on lotto.

And states vary. Most offer longer odds today than 6/49. Puerto Rico Loto Plus is a 5/40 + 1/15 game. Powerball is 5/69 + 1/26.

We have a ticket running in both year around.

Each has an additional draw of one number from a smaller independent pool. There are 26 numbers for PowerBall that runs parallel to Puerto Rico Loto Plus with a 15-number independent pick.

Professors Thaler and Ziemba point out that there are two good reasons rational investors pay attention to lotto.

- The first reason is that some numbers are more popular than others.
- The second reason is that carryover increases the expected value of the ticket from enormous jackpots.

Gamblers are attracted by lifestyle changing jackpots. These people hunger to get rich quick but don't study the game of lottery. They don't use any kind of rational system in the conscious selection of numbers other than the birthday numbers of family members, segments of their social securities or just running a line through a row of a lottery ticket form panel.

Rational investment analysis of the game itself leads to intelligent conscious selection of lotto numbers. Rational investors strive to reduce the probability of splitting the prize. Some rational investors choose to take the time to play only when the jackpot reaches a certain threshold.

Others like myself consider our time too valuable to watch the lottery jackpot size week after week. Hence my wife and I have a lotto ticket running in every Puerto Rico and Power Ball game twice every week of every year.

I'll explain to you how to set up your tickets so that you don't spend more than an hour or two a year implementing the best rational system of playing lotto.

Powerball paid a $1.6 billion jackpot in 2016. This was split among 3 tickets for $530 million each. That's $210 million if winners retained 40% after taxes.

Any family with a $210 million-dollar estate is well at the top of the 1% in America.

That same year, Mega Millions had a payout of $656 million. The Netherlands has had a $46.7 million jackpot.

The Least Popular Numbers in the Lottery

Between 15 and 20 of the numbers are unpopular. Professor Ziemba explains that lotto players frequently pick "lucky" numbers.

Picking lucky numbers is a form of naive conscious selection. These naively selected popular numbers include birthdays.

The highest number in a birthday is 31. That's because 5 months have 31 days throughout the year.

The most popular number is 7. Selecting this number decreases the value of your ticket because your probability of splitting the pot is higher.

Including unpopular numbers in your combinations reduces the probability that you will share the pot if you win. Ziemba asserts that these have edges between 3.1 and 26.7 percent.

Numbers above 31 are unfavorable.

Numbers ending in 0, 9, or 8 are unpopular. The **twelve** least popular numbers per these prominent Ivy League Business School professors is,

1. 10
2. 12
3. 18
4. 29
5. 30
6. 32
7. 38
8. 39
9. 40

10. 41
11. 42
12. 48

These are 15 to 30% less popular than the average number. Those numbers that Professor Ziemba finds are at least two standard deviations below average likeability comprise the nineteen least favorite lotto numbers,

1. 1
2. 10
3. 20
4. 28
5. 29
6. 30
7. 32
8. 34
9. 37
10. 38
11. 39
12. 40
13. 41
14. 42
15. 45
16. 46
17. 47
18. 48
19. 49

Random Conscious Selection

This is best done with a random number generator from within the 19 unpopular numbers. That is because selecting unpopular numbers a priori is a form of conscious selection. Bluskov System #72 can wheel all 19 unpopular numbers above into 26 tickets for syndicates wishing to reduce the likelihood of sharing jackpots.

Random selection eliminates any form of selection bias that arises from conscious selection.

Researchers conclude that there are thousands of combinations that have an expected return greater than the cost of the lotto ticket because of conscious selection of lotto numbers.

Carryover of the pot can increase the expected return to $2.25 per $1 wagered in very large jackpots. For that reason, some players only play when the pot reaches a certain threshold.

I find it more efficient for my wife and I to play a single ticket of a randomly generated set of numbers for 25 games forward. There are 365 days in a year and 7 days in a week.

There are 52.14 weeks in a year.

It costs us $3 to play Powerball and $2 for Puerto Rico Loto Plus for a total of $5 per game. Again, we invest $521.43 per year into the lottery.

We also save $6,500 per year into two Roth IRAs and $24,000 per year into two Roth Solo 401(k) plans.

That is a total of $61,000 saved into our IRA plans.

Our lottery investment program costs us less than 1% of our total savings per year. Yet that small amount is the only hook we have in the water that could turn us into Beverly hillbillies in one lucky evening!

Rational investing households invest in lottery tickets.

They don't play lottery. They look at lottery tickets as call options.

These heads of households sit down as you are doing now and develop a bulletproof system to keep their family in play in lotto 365 days a year. This allows them to buy the cheapest out-of-the-money option with the highest possible payoff — a lotto ticket.

This is what I am showing you how to do now for your family.

Can A Syndicate Make Money in Lotto?

Authors assert that when several factors combine that an individual can have a positive expectation of playing lottery. The first condition is that the unpopular numbers listed above are chosen less and will result in fewer shared wins. The second condition is that ticket values are maximized with very high carryovers. The third condition is that relatively few tickets sold increases the expected value of your tickets.

Just because a lottery ticket could theoretically have a positive expected value does not mean that this will come to pass. There are several reasons that an individual would not likely capture this.

Thaler and Ziemba give the example of a carnival game wheel with a million $1 spokes to bet on. You pay $1 for bets on numbers between 1 and 1 million and win $2 million when you hit. You have a large edge in this game but the likelihood of winning is so slight that you will go bust almost certainly before winning.

I won't risk more than a few hundred dollars per year of our savings for lotto investing for this reason.

Maclean, Ziemba, and Blazenko (1987) form a model that shows that under favorable conditions the $10 million initial stake will grow to $100 million before losing half with probability close to zero. BUT it would take the team thousands of years playing every lotto game in the world to win for sure.

It would take millions of years playing Power Ball.

The founding syndicate members will most likely be many generations dead before the first win. That is if the game is played by each new generation. So, even if unfavorable numbers and large carryovers enhance your edge you will still have miniscule odds as it takes a very long time to expect to win.

Hence, do not expect membership in a lottery pool to increase your probability of winning in any substantial form.

Does it Ever Pay to Buy All Numbers Combinations in Lotto?

Thaler and Ziemba ask the question, does it ever pay to buy all the numbers and hence "steal the pot"? This would only be profitable if there is a large carryover such as $7.7 million on a 6/49 lotto game where few tickets are sold.

This has happened on occasion in minor lotto games.

But this strategy would require enormous effort to redeem so many tickets. A second syndicate stealing the pot would drastically curtail returns to this strategy.

Lotto transaction costs and risks such as this make a "Steal the Pot" strategy untenable.

Explaining the Unexplainable

Payout rates are so dreadful in lottery that nobody should willingly play. Economists are puzzled by the public attraction to this game.

These researchers explain that it is easy to see how a ticket is reframed psychologically as paying 50 cents per dollar for a fantasy of becoming rich for life. Remember that the expected value of a dollar ticket is about half.

Other financial economists have expanded on the definition of the fantasy within the realm of option theory. From that perspective 50 cents becomes option premium akin to a deeply out-of-the-money call option. Read *"Stock Options as Lotteries"* http://onlinelibrary.wiley.com/doi/10.1111/jofi.12152/abstract

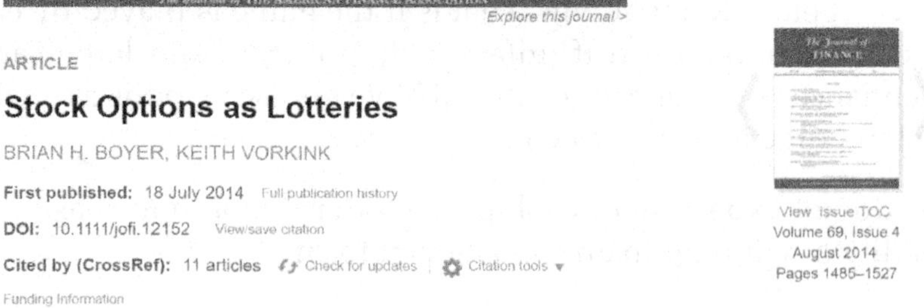
The Journal of FINANCE
The Journal of THE AMERICAN FINANCE ASSOCIATION
Explore this journal >

ARTICLE

Stock Options as Lotteries

BRIAN H. BOYER, KEITH VORKINK

First published: 18 July 2014 Full publication history

DOI: 10.1111/jofi.12152 View/save citation

Cited by (CrossRef): 11 articles Check for updates Citation tools

Funding Information

View issue TOC
Volume 69, Issue 4
August 2014
Pages 1485–1527

The maximum payoff for a lottery option (ticket) is astronomical in comparison to any other available in more conventional capital markets. And yes, lottery is a capital market for governments.

Chicago Booth finance professor Richard Thaler further explains that any expectations that players would continue to choose popular numbers is dashed by arbitrage theory. This says that upon publication of their article in Spring of 1988 in the Journal of Economic Perspectives playing should have shifted away from unpopular numbers.

However, they point to the work of social psychologist Ellen Langer who in 1975 showed that players believe they have better odds of winning when they pick their own numbers — even though this is not true. This she termed the *"illusion of control."* When players pick their own numbers, this is known as conscious selection.

Read: https://en.wikipedia.org/wiki/Illusion_of_control

Lottery players are more reluctant to relinquish their consciously selected tickets as compared to those generated through a random number generator. This is a commonly held mental bias per research in behavioral finance — professor Richard Thaler is a prominent scholar in the field.

The final example in the article is highly illustrative of the bizarre thinking of past winners regarding conscious selection. The winner of the "El Gordo" lottery in Spain said he searched for a ticket with the number 48. When asked "why 48?" the player responded, "Well, I dreamed of the number seven for seven nights in a row, and since seven times seven is 48…"

Investigating the Behavioral Characteristics of Lottery Players

Flash forward twenty-three years to 2011. Professors Rose Baker and Ian McHale published a paper in the Journal of the Royal Statistical Society entitled "Investigating the behavioural characteristics of lottery players by using a combination preference model for conscious selection." You can tell it is British.

Behavioral is incorrectly spelled. LOL.

It is interesting to note how lottery rules change over time. The authors document that in 2011 Powerball was a 5/59 + 1/39 lotto. Nomenclature is that a player chooses a subset of m from a larger pool of M numbers in a m/M lotto.

Today the game is a 5/69; 1/26 format. Selecting all 6 numbers wins the jackpot. The game offers lesser prizes that range from $4 to a million. You expect to win a prize on about every 25th ticket.

Without conscious selection, the probability distribution of winners is an independent Poisson random variable. The Poisson distribution is from probability theory and statistics. This mathematical relationship was derived by French mathematician Siméon Denis Poisson to map the probability of events over a fixed interval of time.

Studies show that the lowest, highest, and average winners reported by Powerball authorities below on their website are unusually high. Conscious selection by inducing more prize sharing violates independence. This results in long tailed distributions of the number of winners and high correlations between some classes of prize winners from sharing.

Match	Prize	Lowest Ever Winners	Highest Ever Winners	Average Winners Per Draw
5 + Powerball	Jackpot	0	4	0.2
5	$1,000,000	0	73	3.2
4 + Powerball	$50,000	2	827	28
4	$100	180	20,544	906
3 + Powerball	$100	490	47,685	1,590
3	$7	11,887	1,164,124	49,299
2 + Powerball	$7	10,526	895,097	28,141
1 + Powerball	$4	69,793	6,343,237	188,318
0 + Powerball	$4	0	14,595,721	400,126
The overall odds of winning a Powerball prize are approximately 1 in 24.9				

Lottery authorities loathe releasing actual ticket numbers purchased in games. They don't want players to know the distribution of conscious selection.

These researchers model conscious selection in the UK National Lotto Game and Spain's El Gordo de la Primitiva.

Direct Evidence of Conscious Selection

Scoggins (1995) discovered conscious selection in the Florida State lottery. The probability of a rollover failed to generate a Poisson distribution.

The six winning numbers for the Canadian lotto on March 19th, 2008 were 23, 40, 41, 42, 44, and 45. The bonus number was 43.

People had simply picked a line in the lotto ticket form.

Without conscious selection of selecting the combination in the lotto form corresponding to 23, 40, 41, 42, 44, and 45 the 5+ prize should have been shared by 3 winners from the 6,606,690 tickets sold. The 5+ prize was shared by 239 winners.

This was a clear violation of the Poisson distribution. Conscious selection arises from;

- 7 is a lucky number in many cultures. On November 14, 1995, the British lotto was shared among 133 tickets for the £16 million prize. This reduced the prize per winner to £120,000. The winning numbers 7, 17, 23, 32, 38, 42 and 48 were all popular numbers with players per the Daily Mail newspaper in the UK. Read the online article entitled "Why *'lucky 7'* really is the world's magic number." This is contradictory to the list by Ziemba showing 42 and 48 to be unpopular.
- Birthdays have a maximum of 31 numbers. Thus, low numbers are chosen more frequently.
- Patterns such as selecting an entire line or block(s) of numbers are commonly selected as I just explained regarding the Canadian lottery above.

Researchers explain that understanding the distribution of conscious selection helps lottery designers rake in more revenue for governments.

The primary conclusion is that if you win using popular numbers you will not maximize the expected value of your lottery ticket because you will most likely share the prize. But you can develop the ability to choose numbers so as not to disadvantage yourself.

The solution is to choose unpopular numbers randomly. That stated, U.K. players have not developed the ability to choose numbers randomly — barriers to arbitrage exist.

Evidence from the Swiss and UK Lotto

Riedwyl (1990) is one of the few researchers to receive the combinations sold in a lotto game. He found combinations with low numbers to be popular. Simon (1999) analyzed data from one draw on October 19 of 1996.

There were 2,000 tickets that would result in a jackpot split among 200 players of the 69,179,660 tickets sold.

The Peculiar Scale Economies of Lotto

The pari-mutuel gambling game of Lotto is one of long odds and large jackpots as explained by economics professors Philip Cook and Charles Clotfelter of Duke University in the top ranked American Economic Review. This is by far the most prestigious academic study of lottery in print.

Here is the background of the study.

A pari-mutuel format is a betting system where all bets are placed in a pool, taxes and the house-take (vigorish) are removed. Then payoff odds are calculated to share the pool across winning bets. The payoff odds are also called the Tote after the totalizator that calculates and displays existing bets.

Examples of pari-mutuel gambling games include horse racing, and greyhound racing. Any sporting event of relatively short duration in which participants finish in a ranked order such as jai alai is pari-mutuel.

By 1989 Lotto was played in 29 of 33 state lotteries. Smaller states operate at a disadvantage in Lotto. Sales increase with state population by $418 per $1,000 increase of advertised jackpot or $500 increase in present value. The actual expected value of the jackpot depends on tickets sold. Instant scratcher lottery sales and illegal numbers games are more inelastic with population.

The Kansas Lottery is an excellent example of instant scratcher class lottery games: https://www.kslottery.com/Games/InstantGamesList.aspx

Consortiums have formed between small and large states.

Mega-Millions is a consortium between 46 localities: 44 states plus the District of Columbia and the U. S. Virgin Islands. For a list of specific states see https://en.wikipedia.org/wiki/Mega_Millions The Mega Millions consortium and Multi-State Lottery Association (MUSL) cross-sell Mega Millions and Powerball in American lottery jurisdictions.

Power-Ball is played in 44 States, Washington D.C., Puerto Rico, and the US Virgin Islands. It is coordinated by the Multi-State Lottery Association (MUSL), a nonprofit organization formed by an agreement with US lotteries.

The likelihood of winning a jackpot is lower the larger the population base. Large lotto games such as Mega Millions and Powerball are riskier. Large jackpots are heavily advertised.

This attracts players to the games with the largest advertised jackpots due to recency bias.

Recency bias occurs when stock market participants evaluate investment performance based on recent results and make incorrect conclusions about how the stock market behaves. This leads to suboptimal decisions.

The expected value of a lottery ticket is lowest after the jackpot returns to the minimum when a large carried over jackpot has just been won. An example of recency bias is when players rush to play small jackpots after a massive payout has occurred.

A large multi-state game plays with the same frequency as a small state lottery. Thus, the larger multi-state population hides the small probability of winning a highly visible jackpot.

This behavior is explained by prospect theory or risk seeking investment behavior. The size of the jackpot matters more to players than the probability of winning.

Because of this per capita lotto sales increase with increasing population.

The Maryland Lotto

Lotto was introduced in 1980 as a state lottery game. The Maryland Lotto was one of the first.

Rules have since changed. But here is how the game was operated at inception according to this study.

A single play consisted of choosing six numbers between 1 and 49. Format is set to match population.

Maryland started with this format offering a 1 in 6,992,000 chance to win. The state population at the time was 4,729,000 citizens.

The product of the probability times the population was 0.7.

The paper shows that states decide the format by population. California lotto started with a 6/53 format. These additional four numbers decrease the probability of winning to 1 in 22,957,000. But the population was much higher than Maryland at 29,126,000.

Thus, the product of probability to win times state population was 1.3. This illustrates the fact that state lotto games set the format to match the state population — the product of probability and state population is roughly 1.

State lotto managers want to reach a balance between jackpot carryover where nobody wins versus multiple winners. As state population rises additional numbers are added to the game to re-balance.

State lotto managers take game format very seriously.

A one dollar bet gives players two plays recorded by computer link to headquarters. A drawing once a week selects the winning combination at random from 13,983,816 combinations. The probability of winning was 1:9,991,908 for each dollar bet.

Any winners share the jackpot.

This is normally paid in 20 installments due to tax concerns. Smaller prizes are awarded to players who correctly select four or five of the six winning numbers.

All prize sizes depend on the total amount bet known as the "handle." Half of the handle went to the prize pool.

Then 79.4% went to the jackpot. The primary reason that investors shun lottery as an investment is that the prize pool is half the handle.

Lottery tickets are poor bets in this light.

State Lotto games share an important characteristic in that the probability of winning the jackpot on a single dollar bet is infinitesimally small. The likelihood of winning ranges from 1 in 974,000 in Delaware to 1 in 23 million in California. Another characteristic of state lotto games is that the size of the jackpot depends on the handle. The third distinction of a state lotto game is that the jackpot winners are prominently displayed to the public to sell more tickets to intentionally increase the handle.

Players face the additional risk of sharing the jackpot. For this reason, you never hear the proposition that a lottery ticket could make sense in your investment portfolio.

Are Lotto Tickets That Bad?!

But, let's take this analysis further. The expected value (EV) of a lottery ticket is,

EV = (Probability of win) x (Jackpot) x (Expected Share of Jackpot if Win).

As the jackpot expands the likelihood of sharing the jackpot rises. But the likelihood of sharing rises slower than the jackpot size as new players buy into the game.

If there is no winner in the first drawing, then the jackpot (and the EV) will be larger in the next drawing.

The expected value of a $1 lotto bet depends on the fraction of the handle and the total amount bet by other players. Many players choose combinations through some process other than the option of having the computer pick numbers at random.

The greater concentration of play on certain number combinations from conscious selection greatly increases the probability of sharing the pot over random choice.

The study discovers one combination in the Maryland lotto drawing that if hit would have split the pot more than 3,200 ways. The jackpot would be whittled to $193.50 for each winner.

What is this nefarious combination of numbers? 1, 2, 3, 4, 5, 6

The main lesson is to focus on large rather than small lotto jackpots in the same game over time. And, strive to minimize the chances that you will share the jackpot should you win.

This course shows you how.

Conscious selection reduces coverage. The number of consciously selected combinations that have been bet in the handle at least once (or not bet at all) increases as compared to coverage under random selection. Researchers note that if at least some players bet randomly coverage increases with the handle and the complimentary probability of a rollover decreases.

But always remember that the advertised size of the jackpot distorts the true value.

Researchers note that, *"people tend to classify small probability events rather crudely as either possible or impossible (Daniel Kahneman and Amos Tversky, 1984 p. 345). If someone wins the jackpot at almost every drawing, then it seems likely that most players will continue to view the new lotto game as offering a real possibility of winning."* Bigger is better for lotto.

Just make sure that you don't increase the amount you play. If you create a system before you play you will avoid over-playing out of excitement of chasing a record setting jackpot.

However, Milton Friedman and L. J. Savage (1948) note, *"it is quite reasonable for normally risk-averse people to be willing to pay a premium (over expected value) for a chance of winning an improvement in their standard of living large enough to cause a qualitative change in their social standing."*

And therefore, you should consider having a ticket in major state and regional lotto games. But you must be systematic.

This course shows you how.

An interesting statistic arises from this study regarding blacks versus whites. Neighborhoods that are predominately black play more numbers games.

An example of this game in New York is named Numbers.

Players pick 1 number from 0 to 9 on three lines. Numbers are drawn twice daily for small prizes.

A comparable game called Pega 3 in Puerto Rico pays a jackpot of $500. Pega 2 pays $50.

Pega 4 pays $5,000.

Lower socio-economic households play more lottery games that have vastly higher probability of winning but miserably lower jackpots. And they don't care about large lotto jackpots. These have no impact and do not draw play away. This is of concern since the expected value of these tickets is also highly negative.

I consider number games to be a form of political predation on the poor.

Nonetheless, a large and growing jackpot correspondingly increases the amount of play. This is true for state and regional lotto games.

Researchers compare this scale affect in lotto to that of insurance. People choose to pay a premium to eliminate the small probability of a large loss with insurance. People choose to pay a premium to create a small probability of a large gain. Increasing the "*scale*" by forming a larger pool of independent risks is useful in reducing investment risk. Increasing scale of lotto is a money maker because it allows players to own a riskier instrument (which is not necessarily perceived as such).

The study concludes that *"large jackpots are particularly appealing to relatively high-income players."* The income distribution of lotto players was higher when the 1980 Maryland Jackpot rose above $5 million.

Final Note: In the case of Powerball if you do not wish to play every game, you should play anytime the grand prize increases to past $146,107,962 (or double that amount if you want the lump sum payout). $(5/55)(4/54)(3/53)(1/51)(1/42) = 1/146{,}107{,}962$

Section 4 • A Players Guide to Lotto Strategies

Rout Out Lottery Cons and Louts!

The article I last explained from the American Economic Review by Cook and Clotfelter (1993) points out a very dangerous inclination, *"Many players do not accept the scientific view of chance but rather believe that the probability of choosing a winning combination in a lottery game can be improved though the application of skill and effort. This belief is evidenced by the active market in advice for choosing lottery numbers, offering everything from numerology texts to news articles that explain what system the latest winner was using."*

This section delves deep into exploring this very real problem through a book by Samuel G. Allen entitled *"A Player's Guide to Lotto Strategies."*

This book is a mathematician's revenge. He describes authors who bill themselves as "experts" in the lotto community with the following four categories,

Scams — These authors victimize the public by over-charging for their expertise.

Self-deluded — This sophist believes in his or her system but is intellectually incapable of grasping the conceptual flaws. A sophist is a paid teacher of philosophy and rhetoric associated in popular thought with moral skepticism and specious reasoning in ancient Greece. Sophists today are highly paid spin doctors for upper echelon politicians as was the case in ancient Greece.

Bad Mathematics — Bad math arises from specious reasoning. It is wise not to learn from those who could not pass 5th grade math. Stupid is as stupid does bad math.

Pseudoscience — These draw from scientifically unsupportable (which is different than unsupported) concepts ranging from astrology to fortune telling.

True lottery experts (which I am not) are published authors from mathematics, economics, or finance. Here is a summary of his review of the quality of authorship in the lottery expert niche. I added Eddie Coronado to the list after reviewing his book.

Book/ Course	Author	Category	Reason
The Lotto Black Book	Larry Blair	Scam	False Claims
lotto-logix dot com winning lotto strategies	Paul Connor	Scam	False Claims
Smart Luck Inc.	Gail Howard	Bad Mathematics	Claims random patterns are non-random.
Winning Lotto Secrets: From a Real Double Million-Dollar Lottery Winner!	Terry Fisher	Self-Deluded	Gambler's Fallacy
Basics of Winning Lotto/Lottery	Professor Jones	Self-Deluded	Gambler's Fallacy
Learn How to Increase Your Chances of Winning The Lottery	Richard Lustig	Self-Deluded	Gambler's Fallacy
Silver Lotto System	Ken Silver	Scam	False Claims
Start Winning the Lottery	Noah Canfield	Scam	False Claims
How to Win the Lottery with The Law of Attraction	Ed Coronado	Delusion	Gambler's Fallacy

Avoid authors in the table when you develop your lottery play system. I do, however recommend that you read each if you are a serious student of lottery play.

Only you can protect yourself from scams. Lifelong research is your best defense.

"How to Win More: Strategies for Increasing a Lottery Win" by professors Henze and Riedwyl on Amazon is a long hard read with the simple conclusion that everybody should buy a quick pick. There is one final important author — the master of lottery wheeling — Iliya Bluskov, Ph.D. I will cover his work in the next section.

Optimal Jackpot Size?

Microsoft engineer Jeremy Elson estimates that the optimal point to enter the Mega Millions lotto is $420 million. He calculates that the expected value of one dollar of play is $0.69 at or above this prize level.

Section 5 • How to Wheel Tickets

Bluskov Systems for Large Number/ Ticket Play

The hardest task I ever set myself to in my life was my doctoral dissertation in market microstructure of the grain futures markets trading across the CBOT. The academic researcher whom I hold in the highest regard in lottery research is Iliya Bluskov. Iliya struggled through a Ph.D. in mathematics working to perfect the optimal lottery wheel.

I recommend any book or course on lottery professor Bluskov publishes. For more information go to https://www.bluskov.com/

Iliya has written the best book ever written on lottery wheels. Miriam-Webster defines a lottery wheel as a revolving drum or hollow cylinder in which lottery tickets are mixed and from which the winning numbers are drawn — also called a policy wheel.

But, Bluskov lottery wheels are different..

His book *"Combinatorial Systems (Wheels) with Guaranteed Wins for PICK-5 Lotteries including Euro Millions and the Mega Lotteries"* published in 2011 has quickly established itself as a classic in Lotto gaming. The purpose of his book is to *"show you the strategies that many big winners, syndicates and individual players alike, use regularly to play the lottery, scooping up some small wins along the way, while waiting for the big hit."*

If you have not ordered his book from Amazon do so now. It is the required text for this course.

The book teaches you how to complete the cycle taking the unpopular numbers you budget for to wheel, play, and redeem.

I will refer to his systems by number only. You must order the book to do the project for this course.

This book will not increase your probability of winning the jackpot. If you lined up a 2,000-mile-long line of pennies where just one was marked underneath as a winner you would still have the same odds of picking a few more scattered pennies and winning.

But this book will increase the joint probability of winning more small prizes. This can help increase the expected value per ticket.

This makes lottery wheeling the meat and potatoes of the lottery syndicate operator.

What is a Lottery Wheel?

Bluskov's doctorate was earned by solving a daunting minimization problem in mathematics. A lottery wheel reduces to the minimum the number of combinations for any given small prize guarantee.

This minimizes your cost of play by reducing the number of tickets you must purchase for a guaranteed win.

The cost of your lottery play can be deducted from your personal return in section schedule A if you itemize. This cannot exceed your winnings.

Hence you cannot make a business out of a lottery syndicate. Keep it family or make it a well-managed club.

The amount of gambling losses you can deduct can never exceed the winnings you report as income. For example, if you have $350 in Lotto winnings but $936 in losses, your deduction is limited to $350. You could not write off the remaining $586, or carry it forward to future years.

Maximizing your winnings through more frequent small prizes eases your income tax burden of lotto play if you itemize. This helps extend your play a bit as does reducing cost.

Per PBS Frontline, *"Of people who gambled [in Las Vegas], the average gambling budget for the trip was $580.90. On average, those gamblers gamble 4 hours per day."*

That represents a loss in savings of $1,161.80 for two spouses.

The lotto play system you are about to learn will take you just minutes per quarter to implement. If you play one ticket in all games annually in your state lotto and the Powerball or Mega Millions draws you will spend far less than what an average couple plays in Las Vegas for a yearly gambling vacation. Your choice between Powerball or Mega Millions depends on your state of residence.

And you will set yourself up for the possibility of winning a life changing jackpot.

Professors Boyer and Vorkink model a lottery ticket as a deep-out-of-the money call in their Journal of Finance article entitled *"Stock Options as Lotteries."*

The optimal strategy is to reduce the cost of these low probability bets.

There is no deep-in-the-money-call trading on any financial exchange with the potential to change the net-worth of your family to the tune of hundreds of millions for a few hundred dollars invested per year. For that reason, Thaler and Ziemba recommend that a lottery ticket be added to a family portfolio.

But this only makes sense if all retirement savings options have been maxed out. If you are not maximizing savings into your workplace 401(k) up to the matching and pumping residual savings into a Solo 401(k) or Roth Solo 401(k) and Roth IRA retirement plan do so first before implementing what I am teaching you now.

The Bluskov Lotto System

The main intent behind this system is to make your lotto play more fun. Bluskov wheeling allows you to involve other members of your circle of family and friends.

Instead of quilting you can invest the same amount of time and money to creating and running a lottery syndicate. You would do this using the 126 systems in the book by Bluskov.

Statistics from the North American Association of State and Provincial Lotteries (NASPL) reveal that 1,136-people won a lottery jackpot of one million dollars or more. And 4,520 people won over a hundred thousand dollars in North American lotteries.

These people won despite the staggering probability of 1 in 175,711,536 chances of nabbing the Mega Millions jackpot. These odds lead people to teach the urban myth that you are more likely to be struck by lightning than win the lottery.

In that same year of 1996 Bluskov explains that just 91 people were killed by lightning. A total of 5,656 large prize winners contradict the commonly held belief that it is impossible to win at lotto.

No Math Needed

The Bluskov lottery systems do not require any math to employ. The textbook for this course focuses on 5 number lotteries. Powerball, Mega Millions and Euro Millions all introduce a bonus sixth number that is drawn from a separate pool.

Players fill out forms on slips of paper with panels for each ticket. Each panel records a combination the player selects consciously. There is an alternative box to check for random number generation that bypasses the conscious selection panels.

A lottery system (wheel) is for players who wish to play more numbers than just 5 plus the bonus.

Remember those 19 unpopular numbers? You can play all of them with Bluskov System #72 that wheels 19 numbers into 26 combinations with 3 win guarantees. See page 211.

Here is how.

A Bluskov lottery system is a well-organized way of playing many Lotto numbers simultaneously in the lotto through use of wheels. Each wheel is a trapping system of mathematical objects with coverings.

The highest covering system offers the best small prize guarantees. This is a fun way for a family to learn about statistical mathematics.

You will only need a lottery system if you play more than 5 numbers in Lotto. The system will organize your selections to guarantee a minimum win for 3 or more numbers you catch.

If you guess 3 numbers correctly out of 19 in system #72 you will have a minimum number of 3 win prizes of 26 tickets wheeled.

Random selection of 26 quick pick tickets guarantees nothing!

Mathematical minimality in the case of a lottery system means achieving a win guarantee in the minimum number of lottery tickets. This is computationally heavy beyond the ability of anybody but a gifted mathematical academic such as Bluskov.

I am a finance professor but this type of combinatorial mathematics is far from my swim lane!

Hence I turn to the work of professor Iliya Bluskov from Bulgaria to help me help you. Most importantly all Bluskov lottery systems are minimal.

This generates the most economical play of more than 5 number selections.

Table of Wins

Bluskov shows you your expected returns through nifty win tables. Lotto is a very large but closed system of number combinations. The table for each Bluskov system gives the distribution of wins in all possible draws. Bluskov systems are well balanced in that almost all the numbers you choose will be nearly equally represented.

This helps you estimate your expected return.

The table shows you your minor prizes if you correctly match 5, 4, 3, or 2 of drawn numbers in a vertical column on the left side of the table. The total number of 5, 4, 3, or 2 wins the system will catch is given in the middle columns of the table.

The right column displays the percentage you catch of total possible prizes.

Remember that Lotto play is a random process. Bluskov can't tell you what the exact distribution of prize you will catch but he can show you the compact range of possibilities.

How to Use the Bluskov Systems

Step 1. Choose the appropriate Bluskov system based on the number quantity you wish to play.

Step 2. Then transpose the system into a spreadsheet.

Step 3. Transpose your numbers into those of the original number system. The spreadsheet will automatically wheel your numbers into a series of Bluskov combinations.

Step 4. Transpose each Bluskov system wheeled combination into playing slips.

Step 5. Triple check playing slips for errors.

Step 6. Withdraw sufficient cash to play slips.

Step 7. Play slips in a Lotto center that is secure. I use Wal-Mart because of the high security. Pocket your tickets and be discrete. Play 3 months forward. Place tickets in a home safe for security. Make photocopy of the tickets.

Step 8. Set up a Google Calendar alert for the last game of play date stamped on the lottery ticket.

Step 9. Replay slips when prompted by Google Calendar. Check winnings before leaving your home. Record winnings on photocopy of prior Lotto tickets.

Numbers can be ordered any way you like. In fact, different ordering will generate different tickets.

You could randomly generate a pattern from the 19 unpopular numbers to further reduce the likelihood of splitting a jackpot with another syndicate that wheels the same sequence in ascending or descending order.

Can You Win Lotto?

Some syndicates try to buy the entire game if a lottery is small enough and the jackpot sufficiently high. But this is expensive even for small lotteries. For large lotto play the cost is prohibitive.

The number of combinations required to purchase every possible combination, a complete system is calculated by,

$$\textit{Complete Wheeled System} = \frac{n(n-1)(n-2)(n-3)(n-4)}{120}$$

Professor Bluskov presents a table that shows that it only takes 126 tickets to cover all possible outcomes of a 9-number lottery. But a lottery of 30 numbers requires 142,506 tickets to buy!

To win a million-dollar jackpot with certainty would take playing Lotto every game twice a week for 2,000 years. Your family progeny would have to play over a million and a half years for the PowerBall Jackpot with odds of 1 in 175,711,536 to expect to win!

That is not good odds. But smaller prizes are much more likely (Bluskov page 21).

Wheeling Bonus Numbers of Double-Pick Lotteries

Bluskov offers a method for wheeling the bonus number in Powerball, Mega Millions, and Euro Millions.

He explains that you can take a small system such as #25 that wheels 8 tickets from 8 numbers and assign one of three selected bonus numbers whether randomly or through conscious selection.

He takes three bonus numbers designated by A, B, and C and creates a 24-ticket system via system #25.

The Isomorphic Copy

The A, B, C bonus number wheeling system can be improved in terms of coverage by creating isomorphic copies of system #25. This is done by varying the sequence of the 8 selected numbers to create three wheeled permutations that generate 24 tickets as before with some of the same sequence and some different. If you play with randomization enough you can generate three fully different permutations of the original system.

A disjoint isomorphic copy of a small Bluskov system such as #25 would give you the coveted benefit of maximal coverage.

Hence if you try to wheel bonus numbers it pays to take the time to try many different input combinations of the numbers you select until you achieve a disjoint isomorphic copy

The number of pairs to wheel bonus numbers is a complete pick-2 system with n numbers. This can be calculated through

$$\textit{number of pairs} = \frac{n(n-1)}{2}$$

Chosen Number of Bonus Numbers	Complete Bonus Wheeling System
3	3
4	6
5	10

You can see that wheeling bonus numbers dramatically increases the number of tickets you play. If you decided to wheel 5 bonus numbers you would have to play 10 isomorphic copies of system #24 that generates 8 tickets. That's a total of 80 tickets required to wheel just three different bonus numbers!

Whether you wheel 19 numbers into 26 tickets or 8 tickets into 3 isomorphic bonus number combinations there is a table in the Bluskov book that will help you decide the system that is best for you. There is a navigation table by quantity of numbers and by number of combinations (tickets).

Finally, Bluskov systems can be combined to give double and multiple guarantees.

Putting it All Together

Maclean, Ziemba and Blazenko (1992) show that a fully Kelly wager per $10 million of fortune is 65 $1 tickets with an 82.7% edge. They claim that this edge can be had by wheeling unpopular numbers to minimize the splitting of the jackpot and 2nd prize. See Maclean, L. Ziemba, W. and Y. Li. 2005. Growth versus security in dynamic investment analysis. Management Science 38. 1562-85.

These researchers describe two lottery games. The first is Case A, a lottery game with a moderate carryover and somewhat unpopular numbers. This is about one in five cases. Case B is a huge carryover and the numbers drawn are extremely unpopular.

The most interesting aspect of this mathematical analysis is that a quarter of the contribution to expected value (CEV) is captured in the lower three prize tiers. Wheeling allows for efficient capture of this value.

The investor would buy 11 tickets for every $10,000,000 of net worth in case A and 65 in case B per this academic study. I have plugged in real values for Power Ball into the table below.

			Lotto Games	
			Case A	**Case B**
Prizes	*Win Prob.*	*Prize*	*CEV*	*CEV*
Jackpot	13,983,816	$ 40,000,000	$ 0.43	$ 0.72
5/6	2,336,636	$ 1,000,000	$ 0.34	$ 0.52
4/6 + B	5,5462	$ 50,000	$ 0.09	$ 0.18
4/6	1,032	$ 100	$ 0.15	$ 0.24
3/6	57	$ 7	$ 0.18	$ 0.18
			$ 1.18	$ 1.83
% Contribution lower 3 Prizes:			27%	23%
Optimal Kelly Tickets to Wheel:			11	65

At the end of the day billionaires could care less about the mathematics of Kelly betting. In fact, I am concerned that if enough people play unpopular numbers that no gain is created wheeling them.

So, I minimize the time I invest by playing one unpopular self-made Quick-Pick in both the Puerto Rico Lotto Plus and the Puerto Rico Powerball twice a week all year long.

I play a full quarter ahead.

However, I do encourage you to at least read the Bluskov book of wheeling systems. You never know when it might come in handy.

I have used his system successfully to wheel Keno tickets in both Reno and Las Vegas. This was a few hundred or over a thousand in several instances in large part because of all the small prizes.

Bluskov has a book specifically for Keno which is an 80-number lottery where a quarter (20) of the numbers (spots) are randomly selected. Players choose numbers in 2 to 20-spot tickets.

I typically play an 8-spot combination and wheel the minor sub combinations of 6, 4, 3, and 2 on a 10¢ ticket. I play that ticket forward for 100 games.

Then I go and have fun. I check the ticket the next day or before I leave.

Caribbean Cash Pot Vacation Plan

A 3 if 5 guarantee is particularly interesting in the only 20 number lotto game in the world. This is in Trinidad and Tobago.

However, you don't have to play all 20 numbers. You can reduce the cost by eliminating the three most popular numbers to play just 17. Per Scientific American the three most popular numbers under 20 are 3, 7, and 8. System #70 offers a guaranteed 3 win if 5 Trinidad/ Tobago Cash Pot numbers are drawn across 18 wheeled tickets.

Cash Pot costs $4 per ticket. That's $72 per game. Five days of Trinidad / Tobago Cash Pot play would cost you just $360.

A 5 day/ 6-night airfare plus lodging deal on Expedia is just $925 at a nice hotel:

https://www.expedia.com/Trinidad.d602649.Destination-Travel-Guides

A five-day vacation to Trinidad would cost you $2,350 for two and about $100 in food and beverage.

Here is a sample of Cash Pot jackpots,

Draw	Jackpot	Winners	Share
5018	$ 127,120.0	4	$ 31,780
5019	$ 157,395.0	3	$ 52,465
5020	$ 165,042.0	5	$ 33,008
5021	$ 165,042.0	6	$ 27,507
5022	$ 168,520.0	5	$ 33,704
5023	$ 216,700.0	10	$ 21,670
		Average:	*$ 33,356*

By wheeling and playing the Trinidad Cash Pot you can provide your family with a comparably priced trip to Las Vegas on the strip. Such a Caribbean Island Cash Pot Vacation could just possibly pay for itself if you hit the jackpot!

Report back if you try this idea.

Lottery and Taxes

You can't incorporate a lottery pool because it is a hobby not a business. And you can only deduct losses up to winnings.

But you can get the syndicate to pay you if you are doing most or all the work. If your syndicate becomes very wealthy and large enough to play thousands of combinations, you should pay yourself as manager for all the work it takes to run your lotto group.

In that case, you can set up an LLC and contract for payment with the lottery syndicate you have formed. Then set up a Roth 401(k) and a solo 401(k) for you and your spouse.

Considerations Should You Win the Big One!

Rule 1: Pay your taxes first. Once you don't owe the IRS, your State, or municipality any taxes, then and only then should you consider giving family members gifts. Follow this IRS guide to charitable contributions before you do anything: https://www.irs.gov/taxtopics/tc506.html

Better yet sit with a competent CPA tax pro such as Jack Cohen in Las Vegas. Google him and it will pop right up.

Rule 2: Take the Annuity! If you should win $1 million dollars you are better tax-wise to take the annual payments of $50,000 each. That's because the lump sum will be more deeply discounted and must pay an enormous tax bill in the first year ... two bad things don't make a good.

Taking payments is a financially intelligent move.

However, you must consider your life expectancy. If you are old or unhealthy such that you do not expect to live 20 years you are better off with the lump sum.

Your family must make payments on all taxes for the remaining payments upon your death. A competent tax attorney such as Jack Cohen CPA will assist you in finding the right answer

Rule 3: Fully fund all retirement options. Make sure you manage your lottery jackpot through a family LLC with wages paid by winnings. This allows you to create and fully fund a Roth Solo 401(k) that should be invested in either the SPY or VFINX or something similar. I cover this in detail in other courses. Make sure you open and fund either a Roth or Standard IRA. If you are over the contribution limit for the Roth IRA [this not the same as the Roth Solo 401(k)] you can make a non-deductible standard IRA contribution and then roll it to the Roth.

Rule 4: Do not exceed the annual IRS estate and gift tax limits. This is $14,000 max per family member other than your spouse. If you exceed this limit you must pay IRS and state gift taxes! Contact a competent tax CPA such as Jack Cohen in Las Vegas Nevada at http://www.yournevadacpa.com.

Rule 5: File lottery gambling losses every year with the IRS. These are limited to winnings which sucks. But it is still a reduction of cost and is explained here: https://turbotax.intuit.com/tax-tools/tax-tips/Taxes-101/Can-You-Claim-Gambling-Losses-on-Your-Taxes-/INF14370.html

Rule 6: Whenever you or your spouse play together with another family member, friend, or colleagues make sure you draw up a group agreement. Per http://lottery.merseyworld.com/Info/Syndicate.html you should include,

1. Agreement date.
2. Syndicate member names, and contacts.
3. Syndicate manager name and contact.
4. Number selection method (conscious vs random) and Bluskov System used.
5. How much each member pays and his or her prize share.
6. Consequences if member cannot pay. Are they out or do they receive a lower share?
7. Publicity management plan should the team win the jackpot. Can members remain anonymous if desired?
8. Distribute all information of who has signed the syndicate contract and who is compliant on payment into the pool. Make it public in a Facebook Group for ease.
9. Specify that the manager will make copies of each ticket and how he or she will keep the tickets safe but accessible.

Rule 7: Seek anonymity. States vary regarding their protection of identity of lotto winners. If you are in a state such as Florida, you will be startled to find your face on a billboard and shocked by the number of ways strangers will seek to take your winnings by panhandling or theft in one form or another. The Red Cross is a good example of a panhandling organization. Stay off their radar through anonymity. Some states offer full anonymity;

- Delaware
- Kansas
- Maryland
- North Dakota
- Ohio

Other states allow for the masking of identity through a corporation that accepts the prize. Check with your state lottery administration.

If you know your state is going to hoist your identity on a pole without your authorization should you win the Mega Millions or Power Ball jackpot and can make a short drive across the border into an anonymous state, you should consider doing so.

You only must drive back across the state border every three months or so. **—Doc Brown**

Disclaimer:

The data contained herein is believed to be reliable but cannot be guaranteed as to reliability, accuracy, or completeness; and, as such are subject to change without notice. We will not be responsible for anything, which may result from reliance on this data or the opinions expressed herein.

Disclosure of risk:

The risk of loss in trading stocks, futures, forex, and options can be substantial; therefore, only genuine risk funds should be used. Stocks, futures, forex, and options may not be suitable investments for all individuals, and individuals should carefully consider their financial condition in deciding whether to trade. Options traders should be aware that the exercise of a long option would result in a futures or forex position.

Hypothetical performance results have many inherent limitations, some of which are described below. No representation is being made that any account will, or is likely to, achieve profits or losses similar to those shown. In fact, there are frequently sharp differences between hypothetical performance results and the actual results subsequently achieved by any trading program.

One of the limitations of hypothetical performance results is that they are generally prepared with the benefit of hindsight. In addition, hypothetical trading does not involve financial risk, and no hypothetical trading record can completely account for the impact of financial risk in actual trading. For example, the ability to withstand losses or to adhere to a trading program, in spite of trading losses, are material points which can also adversely affect actual trading results. There are numerous other factors related to the markets. In general, or to the implementation of any specific trading program which cannot be fully accounted for in the preparation of hypothetical performance results and all of which can adversely affect actual trading results. As costs vary among traders, including commission and fees, hypothetical trading examples usually do not always take commissions and fees into consideration. Please make sure you consider your individual cost of doing business in the form of commissions and fees. For general information on our other products and services or for technical support, please

contact our Customer Care Department at support@worryfreewealth.com.

Made in the USA
Monee, IL
13 September 2026

62981014R00036